T0365842

Love Is . . .

Also by Deeci Murphy

From the N-Side Out
Pork Rinds and Pumpkin Seeds
Spoken Word for the Young Soul
African Animals A-Z a Book of Rhyme and Poetry
Prayer Poems
Spoken Word for the Young Soul
A Familiar Voice

Print information available on the last page.

Rev. date: 03/08/2016

To order additional copies of this book, contact:
Xlibris
1-888-795-4274
www.Xlibris.com
Orders@Xlibris.com

FOR MY SWEETEST LOVE

Contents

Love Is

Love is giving you the last teaspoon of jelly
When you know I can't stand dry toast

Love is sharing whatever I have
But secretly giving you the most

Love is knowing you're so proud of me
And you being secure enough to let me… be me

Love is supporting the things I do
Especially when they have nothing to do with you

Love is worrying about my health
Not hanging around just looking for wealth

That may never ever darken our door
Despite all that you love me more

Love is you taking way too long
Patience with you has made me strong

Love is you making me laugh til I'm delirious
Love is you trying to make up when it wasn't even that serious

Love is the way you always protect
The way you care for me with deep respect

Love is me making you dinner when I really don't want to
Love is you cleaning the kitchen as soon as I'm through

Love is makin sure you've got before anyone else has any
Doesn't matter whether there's a little or a plenty

Love is having your back through thick and thin
Love is not upholding whatever devilment you're in

Love is you loving me, and me loving you for it

Seduction

Your words seduce me as you artfully spin
A story compassionate hoping I will give in

Knowing your power over my sensible mind
Should caution me not to relax and unwind

Swayed and swooned and convinced to comply
Helplessly drawn as I look in your eyes

The seduction is subtle, quiet, and cool
It takes me a while til I know I've been fooled

I could fight it and possibly risk losing out
On an experience worth one day talking about

Is the seduction of me or is it of you?
Hard to tell whose seducing who

Your powerful swagger is warm and enchanting
It has me rethinking and possibly recanting

My decision to not entertain your rouse
Surely I can find some flimsy excuse
To let go and let happen this thing we both want
Stop playing the games as we banter and taunt

My initial thoughts bout your motives are wasted
Erased from my mind after your kisses I've tasted

Gone are my thoughts about your ulterior motives
Counterbalanced by the fact that the chemistry's explosive

If I let you seduce me, it'll be cause I want it
Won't acknowledge the effect of the "extra" you put on it

Won't give you no key, won't ask you to stay
Won't point no fingers when night turns to day

Won't turn this into a full blown production
Let's just call it a mutual seduction.

Freefall

Down into the deepest abyss
A quiet explosion from a tender kiss
You feel it down deep inside the hole
Where you carefully keep your heart and soul
Not just anyone can venture in
You've successfully avoided the possibility for love to begin
You suspect it's time to deconstruct the wall
To let go and soar into that freefall
Love demands that you invest it all
Not hold back or be afraid
Not second guess the decision you made
To love this person with all you've got
Not pick apart what is or is not
They're not perfect, but then neither are you
The gift of love graciously distorts the view
Of what outsiders and onlookers think or feel
It's your heart and it perceives this is real
Commit to love, take the leap
But be prepared, you'll want to keep
The headache, frustration, longing and all
As you soar heart first into love's freefall

If I Tell You I Love You

If I tell you I love you can you envision what that means?
If I tell you I'd do anything for you will you see that as a means to your ends or a way to make
your ends meet;
Or a way to meet me here, right where I am, and begin from there

If I tell you I love you, can you really understand that it's not just a feeling?
It's a constant, a way of being
What you need
Someone to complement, comfort, console, uphold, hold up
I mean hold up wait a minute, respect, admire, look up to and know when I look in your eyes
There is only truth
Cause to bring anything else, is just not worthy of this love

If I tell you I love you can you get THAT or will you see opportunity in this revelation
An opportunity to use my body and not appreciate the offering I bring?
If I tell you I love you can you handle the responsibility that comes with this gift
The responsibility I entrust you with, to make me better, push me forward, not run me over…
or run over me

If I tell you I love you is it too much, or too much love for you to return
To me and only me, cause I don't share, won't share, can't share
What's mine?

If I tell you I love you, can you comprehend what that means or will you see my love as a way
to keep me where you are, or will you encourage me to soar?
Cause if you love me, show me, so I'll know you love me,
and I in turn,
will love you all the more.

Making Time

It's important to spend time alone
No distractions or cell phones
Takin time to just be
Reflecting back on you and me

Before we knew all we know
Back to the days we'd just get up and go
Down to the shore. for a day at the beach
Just me and you within arm's reach

Let's capture a time when it was just us
Before the love, before the trust
Before the kids, the bills or debt
back to the time when we'd just met

We'd work and live for Friday night
We'd go dancing, to set it off right
Did well to remember the strict boundaries that were set
My momma said "you better not let
Daylight's sunrise catch you blind,
Be sure to bring my daughter in here on time
or she'll be yours to keep, no longer mine"

Didn't get that drastic cause it wasn't long before we knew
It had to be permanent, me and you
Made time then, makin time now
Makin sure to honor those vows

There'll always be somethin vying for our attention
But time alone means we won't even mention
The job, the news or family
This time alones' for you and me

And no matter where the path goes from here
Our commitment to "us" is crystal clear
See you and I, we have the key
It's taking that time for you and me

Sit With Me

Sit with me in the stillness of a silent room
Sit with me while I think and daydream
Cause I know my dreams are safe with you

Sit with me through the sadness of disappointments not spoken
Sit with me just because you want to
Your presence alone is a balm of love and affection
And for now….for right now, it's all I need to heal

Sit with me, and hold my hand
Your love speaks to me without words
This silent dialogue is just between us, ours alone
Our bond surpasses and surprises even our expectations
What we share is a strong fortress constructed over trials
and tested over and over through time

So come sit with me, in solitude
And share the tranquility of this moment.

Cry in My Sleep

I cry in my sleep
Awaked by the cool watery seep
Onto my pillow, ever a surprise
Thought all the tears had left my eyes

But, insistent thoughts of you still creep
Recalling the promises you failed to keep
Twists and turns you've taken me through
Emotions paralyzed by thoughts of you

Hope it was worth the pain
The fights, the battles, the constant drain

On our relationship, such as it remains
Estranged and separate, distant at best
If there was a trial, if there was a test

Did I pass? At least make the grade?
I guess I didn't, you never stayed
What a pitiful ending, a sad epitaph
Some things are never meant to be, let alone, last
I can still have you, if only in my dreams
Overwhelmed by the sadness it seems

My tears when awake seem so pathetic
The get over it, move on, you're better off rhetoric

Won't soothe my broken, shattered heart
Can't find the path to make a new start

So I cry…. in my sleep.

Candy Girl

Thicker than a snickers and no doubt twice as sweet
Girl, you look so good to me, good enough to eat

Checkin you out one day, while at a deli in the hood
Hey there Baby Girl, Day-yum... you look so good

I know you think I'm playin jus try'n to pick you up
But when I saw you had to holla, at least say wass'up

If I could get that digit, I mean would it be alright
Maybe we could get together, how about tonight?

I know your mom's be trippin bout men and alla dat
But if we kin git it poppin, it sho would be phat

Face so fine, won't even sleep, yo memory will keep me up
Skin all smooth and creamy just like a Reesee cup

I'm probably not the type of guy with which you usually mix
Did I tell you your skin's a blend of caramel and chocolate
Just like a candy Twix.

Couldn't pass by you, in fact you made me look twice
Eyes bright like Skittles, and girl those hips so nice

I'm a be out cause don't wanna linger here too long
But fo I bounce I hafta tell you you're the kinda girl
I think about when I hear a love song

Now maybe our paths will cross again, then again, maybe not
But if I never see you EVER, trust and believe you are so, so hot

Let's Talk About Romance

What chu know bout romance?
I know it's more than a slow dance

What chu know bout romance?
It sure is more than a lucky chance
Can't sneak up on it in hopes you'll win
For romance you gotta put some serious time in

You sure you ain't getting it mixed with sex?
Romance is something so much more complex

Sex ain't romance you see,
Sex is not what romance is supposed to be
This is where the confusion comes in,
Sex comes in way at the end

Of the kind words, consideration and respect
The tender words and gifts you don't expect
Romance requires a bit of thought
It means complementing me on those shoes I bought
And just so you know,
Romance doesn't work after you get caught

Romance is making me a sandwich without being told
Treating me like I'm special…. you know like gold

Romance is letting me sleep late
It's you fixing and bringing me my dinner plate

What I know about romance is this
It's so much more than a caress or a kiss

Romance is plottin, and plannin and you winnin me
It's bout making sure you keep me where I want to be

Do I know romance?
Intimately

Copper Colored Brother

Copper colored brother

Eyes the palest grey

I see you staring at me

What do you want to say?

You wanna tell me that I'm pretty,

No the word you'd use is "fine"

I fall into that pale grey stare

And imagine you are mine

You approach me slowly,

The world and ground fall away

Losing sense of time and space; is it night or day?

You lay your hand so gently against my waiting cheek

I kiss your palm; sniff your scent, the aroma

leaves me weak

You bring your lips so close to mine

they barely even meet

This tender gesture of affection

Is so erotic, smooth and sweet

Copper colored brother why you standing over there?

Our eyes still locked together in a never ending stare

Just then Mom nudged my shoulder and halted my daydream

Brother proceeded across the street, smiling slightly,

as the waiting light turned green.

Love Liberates

(A Tribute to Maya Angelou)

Love liberates
It doesn't hold
All that tug'gin and
Pull'in really gets old

Love liberates
It doesn't insist
It makes it possible
For you to do as you wish

I can hope you'd want to spend
More time with me
But loving doesn't make that
A requirement, you see?

Love liberates
It makes it o.k.
For me to be here
And you to be away
And feel no insecurity at all about
This love I never want to be without

Love liberates
It doesn't suffocate
It allows us each our own space
Doesn't compare us to one another,
Nor put us in a competitive race

Love allows me to be me
Not a carbon copy of you, you see
It makes room for mistakes, missteps and omissions
Permits a new beginning with no permission

Love liberates
It sets you free
Asks you to accept
The most basic parts of me

No changes needed, no alterations
Content to be immersed in this loving relation
Fully exposed, no barriers, no gates
Hiding behind nothing, cause
Love liberates

An Empty Exchange

Another empty exchange
Coming just shy of the range
Where confidences are shared
Where feelings are spared
Your hearts in a place walled off from my touch
Your standing right here but distanced so much

I used to feel your connection with me
Now I have to be content to just let it be
Cause what we have is all that remains
Of the pieces of us too broken and stained

Never thought love could feel so sad
Never imagined it could get this bad
You say you fear rejection, but so do I
Only it's me who continues to search for the "why"

Deep inside I know I'll never understand
The decisions you made or the path of your plan
We go round about and back again
Only to start back where we both began

Why are you afraid to open up to me?
Can never trust me with the ability to see
The vision of what life looks like to you
Granted I may never see things the way you do

Is it wrong to want real conversations
Wrapped in truth and honesty
Not some rehearsed dialog
You've perfected to a "T"?
I want to stand sure, be certain of your touch
Is this all too needy? Am I asking too much?
I want exchanges from you that are meaningful and real
Want to get the sense there's some substance to what you feel

So do I settle for the scraps thrown off your table?
Or move it along, recoup while I'm able?
Maybe I'll stop looking for what doesn't exist
Just get on with my life and let go of this,
Empty exchange.

Second Thoughts

As I lie here in the stillness next to you

The breath of your back encompasses my view

I think about the gift God has given to me

The years they now number so many you see

I ask myself would I do it again

Or go with my plan to just "live in sin"

Would you have stayed if you weren't married to me?

In retrospect neither of us could see

That we would work and live and raise kids together

So many storms we had to weather

But you kept me safe and warm and dry

Stuck by my side, never to see me cry

Thoughts of things I should have,

Would have,

Could have done,

Second thoughts about you and me,

Not a one.

Wanting

I want to kiss you for the very last time
Pretend we're together and you are still mine

I want to hold you, and hug you, and make believe
The memories of us I'll gladly retrieve

But we both know this is not that
What's transpired between us has faded to black

Cause your with her now, and not with me
You've made it clear this is how you want it to be

Me wanting you as hard as I can
Won't change the fact you're no longer my man

Was there anything I could have done better?
Was I too passive and she the go-getter?

Well maybe so, cause she got you
There's nothing more that I can do

But want, and wait, and hope for a new hand
Who knows what's in the cards, perhaps a new man.

The Sweetness of Love

Like the sweetness of the orange you just shared with me
Our love has grown and come to be

Didn't ask if I wanted it, just needed to offer it you see
Respecting that our needs often intertwine you and me

Cause God gave us a blessed union
An ordained commitment and Holy Communion

Our sacred connection should never be shared
No amount of discretion should ever be spared

Discussing me with another would be an intimate violation
Of our bond, our precious marital relation

We anger each other from time to time
That's no excuse to share what's yours and mine

We bring our stuff into our place
To sort out, make sense, and order our space

But we don't let that stuff cloud our judgment about what is real
Our serious commitment, the way we feel

Our love is much more than fleshly endeavors
Its thoughtfulness, caring, considerate measures

Its time and patience and prayers from above
That's what makes ours the, sweetest love,

Printed in the United States
By Bookmasters